WE

Our Declaration of Interdependence

Unity Prophet

First Edition Published by Robyn Morrison

Copyright © 2024 Unity Prophet

ISBN 978-1-7348132-1-0

We: Our Declaration of Interdependence © 2024 by Unity Prophet is licensed under a Creative Commons Copyright.

CC BY-NC-ND 4.0

This license enables reusers to distribute, remix, adapt, and build upon the material in any medium or format for noncommercial purposes only, and only so long as attribution is given to the creator. CC BY-NC includes the following elements: credit must be given to the creator, and only noncommercial uses of the work are permitted.

Table of Contents

Introduction 4

Religious Influences 20

Our Education 27

Our Leadership Crisis 34

Our Economic Divide 41

Divide and Conquer 53

Our Wicked Challenges 66

Envisioning Our Future 71

Our Declaration of Interdependence 80

Introduction

You are not alone. We are connected. We are never alone.

Our feelings of loneliness, alienation, and division may feel natural. There are plenty of forces at work in our culture that feed our sense of separation. Many of these divisive forces are thousands of years old. The energy ebbs and flows. History is the story of cycles of progress and regression.

The Cosmos is all that is or was or ever will be. Our feeblest contemplations of the Cosmos stir us — there is a tingling in the spine, a catch in the voice, a faint sensation, as if a distant memory, of falling from a height. We know we are approaching the greatest of mysteries. — Carl Sagan

Over one hundred years ago, a new science, Quantum Physics, finally began to explain the interrelated nature of the universe. The divisive forces quickly seized on this new science to create the first atomic bomb, an existential threat to all of humanity.

We exist within the Cosmic web of life. We are stardust, simultaneously insignificant and exceptional. Everything we do or think matters within the Cosmic web.

We far too frequently act and think as though we do not matter. We do matter. We can make a difference for the benefit of the whole. We can also act or think in ways that threaten the whole. We also may believe the world around us is out of our control.

"We" is not the opposite of "me;" it is the whole of creation, and I/me/you are not separate from creation. "We" does not refer to some distinct grouping or category of human beings. "We" shifts our listening from an individualistic point of view to a collective point of view.

"We" is the opposite of "us versus them." In this book, "We" is intentionally used to convey life's all-inclusive, all-encompassing nature. We can overcome the tendency to view life as us versus them.

We are currently experiencing many wicked existential challenges, including the threat of nuclear war, military conflicts, insurrections and coups, gun violence and mass shootings, natural disasters, extreme weather events, extreme economic inequality, and the disintegration or decline of most of the institutions needed to maintain a civil society. Without a highly functioning civil society, "We" cannot thrive.

We are experiencing anxiety at the highest rate in four decades. Increased anxiety is how we, as humans, adapt to a dangerous world. Our anxiety is a wake-up call. We could act like ostriches and bury our heads in the ground, or opossums and freeze up and play dead, or we could faint and fall down like goats. However, humans have more options. In response to wicked threats, humanity and human beings can evolve.

Social media, elected leaders, aspiring politicians, and major corporate media sources collaborate (knowingly or unknowingly) in disseminating intentionally divisive information. Our use of social media and our choice of news sources contribute to our sense of division. We contribute to our divided world whenever we think "they" are causing our problems.

The ostrich, opossum, and goat view threats as external. Humans also have powerful psychological self-defense mechanisms to protect us from things we view as external threats. Our high levels of anxiety correlate with our belief that the causes of our wicked threats are external and that we have no power to protect ourselves. However, most of our wicked challenges are caused by humans. We have the power to address the challenges causing our anxiety because we caused them. We have the ability to evolve.

If only it were so simple! If only there were evil people somewhere insidiously committing evil deeds, and it was necessary to separate them from the rest of us and destroy them. But the line dividing good and evil cuts through the heart of every human being. — Aleksandr Solzhenitsyn

This is one truth we must embrace. Every human is both good and evil. Humans have two powerful primary competing desires; the desire to merge and the desire to separate. Depth psychology sheds light on this internal dissonance and refers to the aspects of our Self that we desire to separate as our "shadow." We make choices daily to share the warmth of our love or the destructive energy of our shadow.

Our highly individualistic culture starves our desire to merge and feeds our sense of self-importance. In Western Cultures, narcissists are rewarded for their narcissistic behaviors.

When someone declares, "I am the greatest," that should trigger an assessment that the individual thinks they are special and separate from the whole. The overuse of "I" and "me" (the first-person point of view) correlates with our global narcissism epidemic. Candidates for political office feel free to claim openly and proudly, "I alone can lead us," "I am the greatest," and "You'll never find anyone as great as me."

Narcissists often project their shadow (negative traits) onto an "other." "I am great. Those people who are critical of me are evil."

When we choose violence, hatred, or greed towards another person or group of people, it is often because we are projecting our shadow. We can be intellectually and spiritually lazy, unwilling to engage in practices that allow us to embrace our shadow, or we can be self-aware, reflective, and willing to integrate our shadow. At this point in human history, we face many wicked threats, and our tendency to project our shadows onto "others" prevents us from doing the internal work needed to create a more compassionate and beautiful world.

There is an old and very wise Native American saying: Every time you point a finger in scorn, three remaining fingers point right back at you. Finger pointing is another phrase that describes our tendency to project our shadow.

The ancient Hebrew prophet Isaiah said:

Then you will call... and God will say, "I'm here. If you remove the yoke from among you, the finger-pointing, the wicked speech; if you open your heart to the hungry and provide abundantly for those afflicted, your light will shine in the darkness." — Isaiah 58: 6-14

We have a collective responsibility to integrate our shadows. We can stop pointing fingers and projecting our shadows onto the latest target group and spend more time and energy allowing the light of love, compassion, and connection to shine for the benefit of all.

Scapegoating is a term that describes our tendency to blame a person or group for the wicked challenges we face. Scapegoating is a tool used to divide and conquer. People greedy for power use scapegoating. It has allowed leaders to project their sins onto the scapegoat(s).

The Nazis scapegoated Jews. Every instance of genocide has used scapegoating to turn ordinary people into mass murderers, killing their neighbors. Leaders use scapegoating to inspire their followers to exterminate the "vermin" in their midst. It has been used so extensively throughout human history that we seem unable to recognize it as part of our shadow. We participate in scapegoating without even knowing we are doing harm.

We may not be aware that we are projecting our shadow. We may be afraid to do our internal work to understand and integrate our shadow. We cannot integrate our shadows while projecting our evil tendencies onto another person or group. We experience a deeply divided world because we live divided lives.

Learning to integrate our shadow (evil side) is our evolutionary task. We cannot know what is true while we are captive to our divided nature. If we think the cause of our suffering is some other person or group, we tend to feel powerless.

When we fail to understand that leaders have historically resorted to divide-and-conquer tactics to control us, we become accomplices in their destructive scapegoating tactics.

Scapegoating always involves lies and projecting the shadow onto the innocent. Since the line between good and evil strikes through the heart of every human being, scapegoating is, in a sense, finger-pointing by masses of people.

Our leaders do not want us to look up the power pyramid. Instead, we are taught to look down on those with even less power than us and blame them for our problems. The truth is that power that is not shared and distributed corrupts. Absolute power absolutely corrupts.

Authoritarianism grants power to a small number of people at the top of the power pyramid, and it believes asserting power over others is the best, or the only way, to organize a factory or large workplace. During the Industrial Age, this may have been useful. In some cases, granting a leader the authority to act on behalf of the community or organization may be useful. We are evolving away from the Industrial Age and need new ways of organizing collective effort.

Authoritarians want to organize a workplace or a political system. Totalitarians want total control over the lives of the masses of people. Totalitarianism is authoritarianism on steroids. Totalitarianism is a system of government (or leadership) under which most people are allowed virtually no freedom, authority, or fundamental human rights. Totalitarians exert ideological control, and scapegoating is how they get masses of people to grant them total power. Fascism and Nazism are examples of ideologically driven totalitarianism.

In addition to scapegoating, totalitarians depend on propaganda and total control over information. Book banning and censorship are always used. Totalitarians must make their subjects fear the "other" more than they fear being oppressed by the totalitarian leader.

People get seduced into following a totalitarian dictator because they fantasize that they will be able to secure a place within that small, very powerful minority at the top. They don't realize the dictator has no intention of sharing power, and anyone and everyone who threatens their absolute power will be knocked off the pyramid or even destroyed.

Before mass leaders seize the power to fit reality to their lies, their propaganda is marked by its extreme contempt for facts as such, for in their opinion fact depends entirely on the power of man who can fabricate it. — Hannah Arendt

We are constantly bombarded with information. Access to and control of information was the defining characteristic of the Information Age and the current Age of Artificial Information. Those of us who are old enough have experienced three distinct phases of the Information Age. The emerging information age has been described as the Age of Artificial Information. All these phases increased the concentration of power by controlling information. Technology that initially appeared to remove barriers, bring the world together, and level the playing field quickly evolved to oppress and divide.

The people at the top of the power and wealth pyramid are not an "other." They are part of the "We." They are playing the capitalism game, hoping to win, without realizing they are also vulnerable to being manipulated and controlled by the algorithms they invented. Technology monopolists have joined forces with or become totalitarians. We assist them in their propaganda and manipulation when we use their social media platform, listen to their podcasts or radio stations, and watch their channels on television. We cooperate in their manipulation.

We now live with the "Internet of Things." The sources of personal information currently mined and used include data from our watches, automobiles, televisions, kitchen appliances, and surveillance cameras. Most of us have no real comprehension of the amount of data collected about us or how it is used to influence and control how we think and spend our time and money.

During the years of the worst spread of the COVID-19 virus, millions of lives were lost, and hundreds of millions will suffer long-term health impacts because of misinformation and intentional disinformation. Of the ten wealthiest people in the world, eight made their fortunes from tech companies. The pandemic made the tech giants unfathomably powerful and rich.

Totalitarians will use whatever tool they can to seize and maintain power. Since the intentional use of propaganda and lies is a core tactic of all fascist regimes, we may look back on the pandemic of 2020-2022 as the fascist plague, not because they manufactured the virus but because they manipulated masses of people in ways that prevented an appropriate response to a massive public health crisis. We must recognize this possibility so that we can be less susceptible to propaganda and lies when the next pandemic spreads. We must prepare because there will be more pandemics in the future.

The most significant gift you can give is to be absolutely present, and when you're worrying about whether you're hopeful or hopeless or pessimistic or optimistic, who cares? The main thing is that you're showing up, that you're here, and that you're finding ever more capacity to love this world because it will not be healed without that. That is what is going to unleash our intelligence and our ingenuity and our solidarity for the healing of our world. — Joanna Macy

Our human minds are capable of extraordinary creativity and wisdom. We developed language to work collaboratively to meet our survival needs and evolve as a species. Humanity evolved through cooperation, not by violence or conflict. Developing language and words was necessary to support cooperative endeavors.

Language can bring us together, but it also separates us. Language functions in part to distinguish "this" from "that." Although the human mind can embrace complexity, our languages have developed to simplify our communication. Simplicity and complexity co-exist. Our language differences constrain our ability to address complexity collectively.

In addition to the Native American proverb about pointing fingers, there is also a Zen teaching, "Never mistake the finger for the Moon." Our language is not the truth—it is merely the finger. The data collected by big Tech companies is not the truth. The truth must be experienced. Words are helpful, yet they cannot replace the complex knowledge available when we fully experience creation, life, or reality. Our sense of connection can be cultivated by fully experiencing creation.

We are moving from the Information Age to the Age of Artificial Intelligence, or the Data Age (where data holds the most significant power and influence). Since our verbal and written language tends to support dualistic thinking, computers and artificial intelligence increase that dualism. After all, computer data is binary. Everything is condensed to combinations of zero (0) and one (1). We live in a highly volatile, uncertain, complex, and ambiguous world. It is ludicrous to believe technology that rises out of a built-in binary will ever be capable of addressing the complexity inherent in the universe. Consider that the sense of overwhelm and confusion we are experiencing is due to an overload of data, which is not helpful information.

Humans are at the top of the power pyramid of all the life forms on earth. Hubris (from Ancient Greek) describes a quality of extreme or excessive pride or dangerous overconfidence and complacency. In Greek mythology, Hubris describes mortals defying the gods or humans trying to be gods. The Greeks believed nemesis (retribution or punishment) was the consequence of hubris. Hubris is the foundation of many myths, and most of the dominant myths of our time involve scapegoating. Some of what we claim as human progress has contributed to our wicked challenges. Hubris would have us celebrate every technological advancement, even ones that create or contribute to our wicked challenges.

When the scientists involved in the Manhattan Project succeeded at splitting the atom to produce nuclear weapons, they permanently changed the nature of our reality. When the Human Genome Project (1990-2003) developed the ability to sequence human genes, it also unlocked the power to create life. Hubris has led us to the point in history where life can be destroyed or created through the technology we created. Our Hubris leads to our nemesis.

Greed, arrogance (hubris), and the lust for power are aspects of the human shadow. They are evil and destructive. Indeed, the line between good and evil strikes through the heart of every human being.

We are taking a journey together as we read this book. We explore the wicked challenges (also described as wicked problems) that we face. The term wicked problem is defined as a problem that is difficult or impossible to solve because of incomplete, contradictory, and changing requirements that are often difficult to recognize. It refers to an idea or problem that cannot be fixed, where there is no single solution to the problem, and "wicked" denotes resistance to resolution rather than evil.

We are using a similar term, wicked challenge, with the same meaning. The use of the word problem creates a closed loop. By definition, these are challenges that cannot be solved. We use challenge or threat instead of problem because, in many cases, we may disagree about whether we are facing a problem or an opportunity. We use challenge or threat because these words create an opening for breakthroughs (challenge) or openings for action (proactive steps to respond to the threat). We will explore the history behind our sense of separation.

In the first chapter, Religious Influences, we will follow the development of ideologies and religion and the rise of the first authoritarians (chiefs, emperors, and kings). Hunter-gatherer and agrarian societies were highly cooperative. Agrarian cultures were settled, and larger groups were formed. In both cultures, extended families or tribes had to collaborate to survive. People were connected to the natural world, and their religious thoughts were animistic. Animism is living with the experience that everything (humans, animals, stones, trees, seas, lakes, rivers, mountains, etc.) is living and possesses a soul, spirit, or anima. These early cultures were not dualistic.

Before the monarchy, women were powerful yet not superior to men. The power hierarchy was not needed. As tribes grew, communication and leadership activities became more complex, and language helped reduce the complexity. Words helped primitive cultures find shared meaning. However, since human beings are meaning-making machines, it did not take long before words created their world. Shared language allowed shared stories, and stories began to shape the culture. Today, our diversity of languages and stories is more complex than ever. We feel divided because our stories and languages shape or define our fractured world.

The second chapter, Our Education, explores how we raise and educate our children as causative factors, or forces behind, the intensity and complexity of our current highly divisive and violent world. How did the evolution from tribes and extended families to our modern-day nuclear family contribute to our world? What is the role of public education in building a civil society with shared meaning?

The third chapter, Our Leadership Crisis, explores the impact of authoritarian leadership on our divisions and our inability to address our wicked challenges or existential threats. We are experiencing a global leadership crisis. Why is our trust and respect for our leaders at an all-time low? Even the CEOs of the largest, most powerful multinational corporations admit they cannot address our global economy's wicked challenges. Why should we trust a small minority of leaders, many of whom realize they are not qualified to resolve the wicked challenges of our time?

In the fourth chapter, Our Economic Divide, we examine the divisive impacts of extreme economic inequality. Over 700 million people in the world lack the necessities of life: food, shelter, clothing, and healthcare. People experiencing extreme poverty face harmful, life-threatening impacts, including malnutrition, low life expectancy, high rates of infant mortality, and an overall lack of safety and stability. In a world where we are all connected, some of us have far too much, while others lack the fundamental things needed to survive. When the small minority of people at the top of the power and wealth pyramid lack compassion, how can the rest of us create a world of plenitude or sufficiency for all?

The fifth chapter, Divide and Conquer, examines the current political environment in the United States, an entrenched divisive and duopolistic system. Money and wealth have always controlled politics in the United States. Yet, the Declaration of Independence, written to inspire the people to take up arms and revolt against the King, includes three basic ideas of democracy: (1) God made all men equal and gave them the rights of life, liberty, and the pursuit of happiness; (2) the main business of government is to protect these rights; (3) if a government tries to withhold these rights, the people are free to revolt and to set up a new government.

The Declaration of Independence was aspirational. It did not describe the reality of the times when it was written.

Once the Revolutionary War was over and it was time to create a new form of government with a constitution, the promises of the Declaration of Independence were broken. Can a nation formed out of violence and division ever evolve into a true democracy? Our Federal Government is disintegrating, and we feel powerless to save it, or perhaps we don't even care.

The sixth chapter, Our Wicked Challenges, provides a cursory overview of a few additional complex challenges that we have been unable to resolve due to our deep divisions. Zeitgeist is a word that comes straight from German - Zeit means "time," and Geist means "spirit"; the "spirit of the time" is what's going on culturally, religiously, or intellectually during a specific period. The zeitgeist is a phenomenon of "We." We create and participate in the zeitgeist. We exist within the zeitgeist. We are experiencing complex wicked challenges. Those experiences are individual as well as shared.

How do we address our wicked challenges in a post-truth zeitgeist? Our current zeitgeist is one of paradox, contradiction, and confusion. A paradox presents conflicting ideas and relates them in a way that forces you to wonder if it's true or false. One example of the paradox of the current times is the "anti-woke" movement. The initial meaning of the term "woke" described becoming more aware of social injustice. As time passed, the term began to be used recklessly. People subject to the oppression of social injustice and advocates for social justice began to use the term to separate themselves from others who were not woke. Underneath that separation is our typical us-versus-them struggle.

Those who participate in supporting racism or deny the existence of racism and other forms of social injustice began to feel criticized by the term woke. Leaders stepped in, using "anti-woke" as powerful propaganda and scapegoating tool.

The term woke, originally used to promote greater tolerance and understanding of the impact of social injustice, divided people into us and them. The desire to promote tolerance created a backlash against tolerance.

This is a classic paradox of tolerance. Beneath the conflict between woke and anti-woke, there is a conversation about tolerance. We must be intolerant of intolerance to remain tolerant. This is only one wicked paradox based on the language we use that is actively dividing us.

In the seventh chapter, Envisioning Our Future, we turn toward the future. People all over the world are fearful of what we sense is coming. The apparent economic, political, social, and environmental trends are frightening. During the global pandemic, some of these paradigm shifts began to accelerate. We prefer slow, incremental progress. However, a review of human history suggests that evolutionary progress is often dramatic and sudden. History rises out of massive social breakdowns and breakthroughs. Every new generation shapes the world. New inventions create dramatic technological advances. We can be hopeful about our future.

We have strong mental filters. These cognitive devices help us survive but make us closed-minded and even stupid. Our confirmation bias restricts our wisdom, so we reject new ideas or information if it conflicts with what we already know or believe. The belief that we experience the real world, our reality bias, keeps us stuck in what we already know, leaving us with huge blind spots.

Like the Captain of the Titanic, we only see the tip of the iceberg and conclude that something that small is not a threat. The biggest threats are usually invisible until it is too late to change course. Our power is limited unless we become part of a larger movement.

Never doubt that a small group of thoughtful, committed citizens can change the world. Indeed, it is the only thing that ever has. — Margaret Mead

We far too frequently act and think as though we do not matter. We also may believe the world around us is out of our control. We do matter. We can, and we do, make a difference for the benefit of the whole.

We live in an age where one person with control over nuclear weapons can destroy life on Earth. Yet, mass movements of people working together can transform the world for the better.

When we overcome thoughts of separation, resist scapegoating, and stop projecting our shadows, we can create a world that works for all living things. The secret is that we need to join or create movements with other people.

Our book ends with Our Declaration of Interdependence. We are called to live into this bold declaration, moving beyond notions that our freedom is gained through independence.

Religious Influences

Since God is One and all things in heaven and earth are created by God, heaven and earth must be One as well. — Ilia Delio

How did our experience of being separate and not connected first begin? Primitive tribes did not have that experience. They felt deeply connected to the world, other humans, and the non-human world. How did that change as humans evolved?

Hunter-gatherer tribes collaborated and developed effective survival strategies. Humans collaborated with other humans and began the most ancient and longest human-animal collaboration with dogs. Humans were dependent on the non-human world.

There were many incomprehensible blessings and threats that shaped their experience of a power greater than themselves. Humans have always created meaning out of experience. Humans believed they were integrally connected to plants, animals, and their natural environment. Animism is the term anthropologists have used to describe this ideology as the belief that all living things have a soul. Hunter-gatherer tribes did not experience any separation between heaven and earth.

Religion progressed from animism to polytheism. Polytheism is the belief in, and often worship of, multiple gods, deities, or spirits. Ancient Greek, Roman, German, Celtic, and Norse people worshipped gods, goddesses, spirits, and deified mortals (both god and human). Zoroastrianism (the religion of the Ancient Persians) was the first to define an afterlife. The concept of monotheism, as we understand it today, did not exist in ancient times. Ancient people were polytheists. They may have elevated one god as higher than the others (henotheism), but they recognized the existence of divine multiplicity.

The sky was the domain of the polytheist gods and goddesses. Many of these more-than-human characters had the power to transcend (cross over) from the sky to the earth. They could also travel to the underworld. There was no central authority or book. Myths and legends about the various gods and goddesses were passed down from generation to generation through stories. Groups developed rituals and practices to worship or influence the gods. Many of the rituals were closely tied to the seasons and cycles of life.

The earliest of the three modern Abrahamic religions, Judaism, developed within a predominantly polytheistic culture. Initially, the ancient Jewish people (Hebrews) practiced a nomadic tribal religion. There is evidence that ancient Hebrews regularly acknowledged the existence of other gods. However, their religion discouraged any form of worship of any gods or spirits other than Yahweh. Yahweh rescued them from captivity as Egyptian slaves. Yahweh was their god. They were Yahweh's chosen people.

The transition to monotheism occurred when the Hebrew people were exiles and captives of the Babylonian Empire. A small group of priests and scribes created monotheism to unify the scattered, exiled Hebrew people. These priests and scribes gained power by asserting that Yahweh (their God) was the only God; this one God chose the Hebrew people above all other people.

In our time, Christianity is the largest world religion, and Islam is the second largest. Judaism is much smaller, but all three trace their history to Abraham. They are called the Abrahamic religions, and all practice some form of monotheism. There has been a consistent correlation between religious beliefs and social division that can be traced back to the rise of monotheistic religions.

Ironically, these three religions trace their origins to Abraham, and all have compassion and love (including for enemies, foreigners, and strangers) as core teachings. Jesus taught his followers that the very nature of God is love and that we are called to love one another. One of the core teachings of Islam is compassion. Moses, David, and the ancient Jewish (Hebrew) prophets also taught love and compassion, including compassion for travelers and foreigners. The Prophet Muhammad was known for his compassion towards everyone and taught his followers to do the same. Muslims are encouraged to show compassion towards all living beings, whether humans, animals, or plants.

It is hard to deny the correlation between religious beliefs, violent crusades, and religiously motivated warfare. A connection between extreme religious beliefs and violence is present in our current wars. Yet nearly all the major world religions emphasize love, compassion, patience, tolerance, and forgiveness. How do we make sense of this dichotomy?

Christians and Muslims were both involved in conquests, crusades, and violent support for colonization by empires. Historically, Jewish people were more likely to be persecuted and less likely to force their beliefs on people violently. Are there beliefs that are common within Christianity and Islam that can shed light on the intensity of our divisions and the resultant violence throughout the world?

Religions and ideologies are both systems of belief. All religions are ideologies, but not all ideologies are religions. Feudalism, authoritarianism, globalism, capitalism, fascism, communism, and environmentalism are just a short list of the ideologies that have shaped our experience of the world as divided. One belief is common in many of our current ideologies: a fundamental belief in the separation of heaven and earth. Monotheism inherently separates the universe into the sacred (God/Heaven) and the profane (humans, the earth, and material reality). God exists outside of the physical world. God is distant, and we need religious intermediaries (preachers, priests, or popes) to know and understand God.

Monotheism developed within ancient Judaism as a belief system that was core to their story of escaping slavery and successfully conquering and claiming land (modern-day Israel, Palestine, Gaza, and the West Bank) home to competing nomadic tribes. Using violence to seize land from nomadic tribes as a God-given right would be repeated in the Americas and other parts of the world.

Monotheism not only inherently separates the universe into the Sacred and Profane; it is also an ideology that separates God from the earth. Early monotheism was not only an ideology that fueled violence and the conquest of nomadic lands; Abrahamic religions interpreted the distance between God and the earth as a transfer of power over the natural world from God to humans. The notion of original sin is a religious explanation for the dual nature of human beings. God was good. Humans were bad. Humans made sacrifices (other humans and animals) to appease God and overcome their sinful nature. Colonizers felt righteously justified in forcing indigenous people to convert to save their lives as well as their souls.

With the displacement of God from the earth and the natural world, at the same time, as the social structure became more complex, hierarchies of power developed. The first hierarchy was the suppression of the female goddess and women. Polytheistic religions recognized masculine gods and feminine goddesses. There is also substantial archeological evidence that agrarian and pastoral societies revered the Earth as their mother/creator. Monotheists needed to displace the goddesses and all the gods who did not show a preference for their tribes or people with one all-powerful God.

Since the ancient Israelites believed in one God (separated from the earth), God became more distant and unapproachable. God was no longer experienced as dwelling with humanity in the natural world, the changing seasons, or the cycles of famine and abundant harvests. Humans needed an intermediary to please or experience this distant god. Soon, there were Priests and Kings and hierarchies of power. The Priests and Kings demanded sacrifices from the people.

The Hebrew people were required to give part of their harvest or herds to their religious or political leaders. Priests also demanded the ritual sacrifice of animals, preferring the best of the animals, the beginning of the use of scapegoats. A perfect lamb was slaughtered to atone for the group or tribe's sinful nature. The sacrifice of the innocent scapegoat served to appease God and save the rest of the tribe.

A scapegoat remains effective as long as we believe in its guilt...
Learning that we have a scapegoat is to lose it forever...
If you scapegoat someone, it's a third party that will be aware of it. It won't be you. Because you will believe you are doing the right thing. — Rene Girard

Scapegoating has always been a powerful and effective tool of hierarchical power. It evolved into a system of power-holders blaming innocent people (including groups and categories of people) for the circumstances and complaints of the mass of people. The scapegoat had to be eliminated from the tribe either by driving them out into the wilderness to die or by ritual killing.

Because we evolved from animism to monotheism, organized religion and politics have historically been intimately connected by a common thread - both ideologies require power over people by a small minority. The separation of the sacred and profane created the divide between heaven and earth. Religious leaders inserted themselves between the people and their God, requiring obedience and submission to systems of oppression and division. Monotheism became one of the roots of our sense of separation.

We are not separate. God is not distant. We do not need hierarchies of power to experience the presence of the holy or the sacred. The sacred and the profane are always with us. All living things are sacred. We were created to love creation, including all that is. When we open our hearts and minds to this experience of unity, we are free to love it all. Everything becomes holy and sacred.

Love is the most universal, the most tremendous, and the most mysterious of the cosmic forces... the physical structure of the universe is love. — Pierre Teilhard de Chardin

Our Education

Education is the most powerful weapon which you can use to change the world. — Nelson Mandela

What is the role of public education in creating and sustaining a world of unity and cooperation?

A population with better education has less unemployment and reduced dependence on public assistance programs. Education reduces crime, improves public health, and fosters greater political and civic engagement. It is hard to imagine what our world would be like without public education's contributions to human development and the tapestry of civil society.

Our world has grown increasingly complex. Only one in four CEOs of the largest multinational corporation believe their organizations' leaders have the knowledge and capabilities to manage the current volatile, uncertain, ambiguous, and complex (VUCA) world. The problem is not a lack of knowledge. Our public educational system was not designed for the VUCA world. Public education was developed during the Industrial Age to develop people who could successfully perform repetitive tasks. The emphasis was not on developing creative problem-solving skills.

How best to educate our children is one of the most divisive issues of our time. Teaching has always been political. Public education is a tool to shape a civil society. Public education has historically used a didactic style. The teacher gives lessons to students in the form of a lecture. Students listen and memorize the information. There is minimum interaction between the students and teachers. The students are not encouraged to form their own opinions and thoughts. Although most teachers strive to be neutral and teach the facts, bias is an inherent trait of didactic education.

As we shifted from the industrial to the information age, public education evolved and began to emphasize critical thinking and creative problem-solving. At the same time, more parents began to choose home-schooling or private schools. General support and funding for public schools also decreased.

Publicly funded and governed education is threatened, negatively impacting the primary goal of public education. We cannot experience the stability and power of a civil society without quality, community-supported, citizen-governed, and publicly funded education.

Current fights over our public schools, including fights about curriculum and the books that belong in the school library, are often arguments between us and them. We have strong opinions and little or no consensus. Our neglect of public education over the past generation contributed to our inability to address our wicked challenges.

Is it possible for a deeply divided society to create an unbiased educational system? We disagree about what is true. We have different values and beliefs. We live in a post-truth world, or a world of misinformation.

Given the intensity of our social and political divisions, there is no consensus on what we should teach our youth. Neutrality, or resistance to any change is a political choice that bolsters the current power structure while marginalizing and ignoring many students' fears, interests, and concerns. We are diverse, and so are our children.

One of the primary objectives of public education has been to prepare people to do repetitive work. Public education was partly hierarchical because it was designed to shape minds to follow instructions or orders. The emphasis on standardized test scores was well-intentioned. However, it solidified a culture of right- versus-wrong thinking. Even multiple-choice tests narrow the options. There have been educational programs that encourage creative thinking, but funding for those has decreased over the past decades.

Although a small percentage of private schools provide excellent models of student-centered civil society-building education, most are reactionary efforts to indoctrinate students in authoritarian or religious dogmas. Often, private school curriculum encourages and supports civil divisions. Authoritarian religious education frequently employs scapegoating to intentionally teach students they are better than other people and, even worse, that other people are evil and destined to go to hell.

Didactic teaching supports power hierarchies: the teacher is more powerful than the student. Didactic teaching supports right versus wrong thinking. This core dualism thwarts the imagination and creativity of our children. It also explains the distress some parents experience when their children are didactically taught one version of history, especially when it is not the history they were taught; or the history does not accurately teach the experience of their ancestors.

A paradigm can be defined as a worldview or viewpoint of reality. Paradigms are complex frameworks of assumptions, values, practices, concepts, and rules that shape our thoughts and actions. Paradigms operate primarily out of our subconscious. When we educate our children, deeply rooted, primarily subconscious paradigms develop that influence their adult lives. Public education forms, shapes, and transforms paradigms.

We don't have a shared public school system. We have public schools, private schools, and home-schooling. These educational systems contribute to deeply divided paradigms. We feel separate because our education and upbringing have shaped us with differing and competing paradigms. These paradigms drive our cognitive dissonance and other psychological self-defense mechanisms. When we are defended, we are not experiencing our WE. When we remain open, our paradigms can change quickly and dramatically.

You could say paradigms are harder to change than anything else about a system, and therefore this item should be lowest on the list, not second-to-highest. But there's nothing physical or expensive or even slow in the process of paradigm change. In a single individual, it can happen in a millisecond. All it takes is a click in the mind, a falling of scales from the eyes, a new way of seeing. Whole societies are another matter—they resist challenges to their paradigms harder than they resist anything else. — Donella Meadows

The primary obstacle to addressing humanity's existential or wicked challenges is our inability to collaborate with people with different subconscious paradigms. Paradigm pluralism in public education has the power to transform our world. Fostering a publicly funded educational system that promotes paradigm pluralism is the most effective lever to resolve our wicked challenges.

We need only look at changes in educational policy since the 1990s to understand how the shifts in educational paradigms create social transformation. As our economic world shifted from the industrial to the information age, we started emphasizing S.T.E.M. (Science, Technology, Engineering, Mathematics) education.

The acronym S.T.E.M. was coined in 2001, at the technology bubble's peak. One of the benefits of the S.T.E.M. emphasis in public education was it involved students in more complex projects where they had more opportunities to apply their knowledge.

One of the challenges was the emphasis on S.T.E.M. education, which led to a neglect of other subjects, decreasing the emphasis on civics, history, music, arts, the humanities, social studies, and the natural sciences. The increasing emphasis on S.T.E.M. also correlated with a rising gap between average compensation in the technical fields versus caring careers (teaching, childcare providers, caregivers, and social work). Since women have typically dominated these caring careers, the emphasis on S.T.E.M. partially explains our inability to decrease the lifetime earnings gap between women and men, even as more women entered the full-time workforce.

If men make more money than women, then patriarchy maintains power over women. Perhaps the emphasis on S.T.E.M. contributed to our increasing inability to understand

and have compassion for other people. Maybe it even contributed to increasing military spending, especially given the impact of technology on our war strategies.

The emphasis on S.T.E.M. as the dominant educational paradigm fueled the Age of Artificial Intelligence. Ironically, Artificial Intelligence will likely reduce the need for S.T.E.M. workers even more dramatically than caring workers. The future educational paradigm must incorporate and celebrate our diversity.

Recently, educators have coined the term S.H.A.P.E. as an additional educational paradigm. S.H.A.P.E. refers to education that offers Social Studies, Humanities, and the Arts for People and the Environment or Economy. Combining S.H.A.P.E. plus S.T.E.M. is genuine educational pluralism, education with the power to overcome divisions and address real-world challenges. S.T.E.M. brought us the Age of Artificial Intelligence. S.H.A.P.E. plus S.T.E.M. will give us the power to use technology for the common good.

Educational pluralism acknowledges four principles.

1. Quality education is a common good. It is valuable for individuals and the community.
2. Education is not neutral. Children learn facts and information as they grow up, but their character also matures and develops. Education shapes our mental paradigms.
3. Quality education must be accessible to all children and their families, not just the wealthy.
4. Educational pluralism advances academic achievement (test scores, etc.) and develops a workforce capable of thinking outside harmful narrow or dualistic paradigms. It

will create a workforce capable of addressing our wicked existential challenges.

A world where everyone knows we are all connected, and our lives are interdependent needs an educational system that educates our children for the common good and honors our diversity. Children need to learn to appreciate differences in religious, cultural, ethnic, and racial backgrounds to overcome the harmful impacts of scapegoating.

A genuine appreciation of differences would result in fewer wars and mass shootings. Most of the world's democracies (the U.K., Belgium, Sweden, the Netherlands, and many Canadian provinces) already offer educational pluralism paired with robust regulations and a common core curriculum. We know publicly funded educational pluralism is possible and effective in building a civil society.

The function of education is to teach one to think intensively and to think critically. Intelligence plus character–that is the goal of true education. — Rev. Dr. Martin Luther King, Jr.

Our Leadership Crisis

The need for new leaders is urgent. We need new leadership in communities everywhere. We need leaders who know how to nourish and rely on the innate creativity, freedom, generosity, and caring of people. We need leaders who are life-affirming rather than life-destroying. Unless we quickly figure out how to nurture and support this new leadership, we can't hope for peaceful change. We will, instead, be confronted by increasing anarchy and societal meltdowns. —Margaret Wheatley

We are in the midst of a global leadership crisis. Respect for leaders (in all sectors of our society) is at a historical low. Why don't we trust or respect our leaders?

Power and decision-making authority are concentrated at the top of our organizational hierarchies. Top-down didactic education contributes to our deep divisions and the divisions we experience in all sectors of our society. Top-down leadership decisions are siloed; they are made from specialized or narrow perspectives. This traps us in a narrow-minded and even closed-loop problem/solution cycle. We were taught that there are right and wrong answers, and we approach complex problems with that same mindset.

We live in a Volatile, Uncertain, Complex, and Ambiguous (VUCA) world. There are many existential threats (wicked challenges) facing humanity. Our dominant paradigms created or contributed to these wicked challenges. We have made decisions using technical dualistic thinking that traps us in the problem-solving cycle. We have been working on these wicked challenges in a cyclical process. A group of people get together to solve a problem, and the solution leads to new problems that need more solutions.

Another way of looking at this is to describe the issue not as a problem but as a situation that motivates people to gather to find ways to transform the situation. For example, the situation with gun violence and mass shootings. One group of people gathers to solve the problem by placing armed guards, arming teachers, and allowing older students to carry guns to school. Their mindset or paradigm is that more guns are the only way to protect lives. Another group of people gather to solve the problem by regulating and restricting access to guns. Their mindset is that too many and the wrong types of guns are the cause of the violence. The two factions oppose each other, and no progress is made.

Another example is addressing the human causes of our current climate crisis. One faction blames the fossil fuel industry and promotes electric vehicles and solar energy. Another promotes a vegan diet to decrease the negative impacts of mass meat production. Another completely denies that we are experiencing a climate crisis. Any incremental changes arising from siloed approaches to complex threats will always be inadequate.

Wicked challenges cannot be transformed by the traditional problem-solving approach because there is generally no clear understanding of the situation. The first issue may be defining the situation as a problem because diverse groups of people may interpret the same situation differently because of their psychological filters.

Wicked challenges include issues like extreme poverty, hunger, environmental degradation, nuclear weapons and power, increasing natural disasters, terrorism, migration, housing scarcity, pandemics, decreasing birth rates (aging population), decreasing life expectancy, and deteriorating public health. Wicked challenges can be systemic and ongoing or abrupt and urgent. Wicked challenges are inherently complex. They are also volatile, uncertain, and ambiguous.

The 2020 COVID-19 pandemic is one example of an abrupt, wicked challenge. A tiny virus quickly brought the world to the brink. There was no consensus or shared reality with the pandemic. The pandemic triggered primitive emotions: fear, frustration, boredom, altruism, selfishness, and distrust. Humanity reverted to our lemming or lizard brain, the part of our brain that automatically controls fight, flight, feeding, fear, and freezing up. The lemming analogy fits the best. The myth of the lemmings is that they follow each other off tall seaside cliffs when their population becomes unsustainable.

COVID-19 produced a corresponding pandemic of disinformation. Discerning the truth about the disease or the vaccines developed to help us survive was nearly impossible. COVID-19 created mass moral panic. Panic can be as contagious as any virus. Panic can also be deadly.

Given that the global leadership crisis preceded the COVID-19 pandemic, we did not have the leaders or the confidence in our leaders to guide us through a dangerous time. Nations and states had different experiences of the pandemic because they had different kinds of leaders guiding them.

Although not all states struggled equally, overall, the response of the United States was abysmal, given that US taxpayers primarily funded the science behind the development of the vaccines. The then President of the United States had no knowledge or skills about how best to react to the threat. He ignored public health experts. His primary concern was his ratings and popularity. The United States also developed the internet and most social media platforms, which proliferated false information and mass confusion.

The deep paradigm divisions within the United States prevented our leaders and individuals from effectively responding to the complex threats surrounding the COVID-19 pandemic, which was a VUCA event.

It is time to reconstruct national and international relations between people and leaders. It is time for leaders to listen and show that they care — about their own people and about the global stability and solidarity on which we all depend. — António Guterres

Social media and technologies were unable to help us during the pandemic. We sometimes think technology and artificial intelligence will solve our wicked challenges. Yet, our experience during COVID-19 demonstrated the inherent weakness in the world of unlimited bits, bytes, data, and algorithms. There was no consensus about what was true and what was false. We were overwhelmed with information and data and unable to access sufficient emotional intelligence— the greater the divisions within a nation, the less effective the decisions made by the leaders.

Social media (Twitter, Facebook, Instagram, and others) profited from the pandemic. This was not surprising because their business model intentionally profits from dividing us.

Although they benefited from record profits, they refused to allocate resources to remove false information or conspiracy theories. Hundreds of thousands of people died unnecessary deaths, and millions will suffer health consequences from the long-term effects of their COVID-19 infection because social media created irrational fears about solid-tested medical science. Public health and medical professionals' lives were threatened by people who consumed and believed false information that went viral on social media.

The concentration of power by a handful of global technology and social media CEOs has become a wicked challenge. The Masters of the Technology Universe (the tech CEOs) have a common distinguishing characteristic: grandiose narcissism. Grandiose narcissism is a mental state characterized by exaggerated feelings of superiority, entitlement, self-importance, an obsessive need for admiration, and a lack of empathy towards others. Elon Musk is a classic example of grandiose narcissism. Adolf Hitler and Vladimir Putin also fit the description. Studies have shown much higher percentages of grandiose narcissists at the CEO level of multinational corporations than in the general population. It makes sense. You don't get to become one of the Masters of the Universe by sharing and caring.

There is no correlation between narcissism and intelligence. We should not assume that the Masters of the Universe are more intelligent than we are. On the other hand, there is a correlation between narcissism and low EQ (emotional intelligence). A narcissist thinks only of themselves and their personal interests. They are unable to understand the needs of others. They already think they are better than other people, so they rarely try to improve their people skills. Narcissists exhibit poor interpersonal relationships. Their excessive need for attention tends to draw followers, not peers. The narcissist views their followers as extensions of themselves. They cannot discern their followers' needs, which leads to less pro-social behavior—the negative traits of a narcissist increase whenever their ego is threatened.

Which came first? Is it the narcissist characteristic of the CEOs, or is there something inherently divisive about the technology? Social media and the rise of a new wealthy class of social media influencers correlate with a sharp increase in narcissistic behavior among adolescents. Facebook, Instagram, TikTok, and Twitter are particularly problematic because they intentionally encourage the oversharing of personal images (selfies) and opinions.

Younger generations who have never experienced a culture without social media are the most vulnerable to social media's intentional divisiveness and narcissism, which consume so much of their time. The mental health costs of spending more time online (and on their phones) have also increased depression and anxiety. The use of social media affects young people in different ways. The higher a youth is on the narcissism spectrum, the more likely they are to have positive feelings about their social media life.

Vulnerable narcissism can be distinguished from grandiose narcissism in part by where the person lands on the introvert/extrovert and direct/indirect continuums. Young people with vulnerable narcissism are more likely to lack self-confidence and are more covert in displaying their narcissism. Grandiose narcissism is characterized by dominance, self-assurance, and aggression. Grandiose narcissists are more likely to become social media influencers. Vulnerable narcissists may engage in constant comparison, judging themselves harshly, feeling that they don't measure up, and feeling envious and resentful.

There is a frightening correlation between mass school shootings and social media. A mass shooter is more likely to fall high on the narcissism spectrum. The strongest correlation between mental health and mass shooters is an extreme sense of superiority. Many mass school shooters fall into the vulnerable narcissist category. Their resentment and envy can lead to revenge shootings that end in suicide. Grandiose narcissistic mass shooters crave attention and seek notoriety. We should not mention the names, share photos, or share the manifestos of mass shooters because that publicity tends to inspire other malignant narcissists.

The negative impacts of social media on young people must be added to our list of wicked challenges. This is one wicked challenge that could be transformed into a positive. A critical wicked challenge is allowing younger generations to reap all the positive benefits of technology while mitigating or removing the dangers.

We must act quickly to address the wicked challenges and opportunities artificial intelligence and social media present.

Over time, the implications of these technologies will push humanity to navigate a path between the poles of catastrophe and dystopia. This is the essential dilemma of our age… The only coherent approach to technology is to see both sides simultaneously. — Mustafa Suleyman

Our Economic Divide

We can create a world that works for all living things. There is enough for all. Our thoughts of scarcity and economic security relate to our current extreme economic inequality. We fall victim to thinking there is not enough for everyone. There could be, but collectively, we lack the imagination to create equitable economic systems.

Plenitude, a word first recorded in the 15th century, describes a situation where there is enough. Plenitude is the universe's natural order, yet we do not all experience plenitude.

If plenitude is the natural state of the world and even the universe, then why do over 700 million people in the world lack the necessities of life — food, shelter, clothing, and healthcare? People experiencing extreme poverty face harmful, life-threatening impacts, including malnutrition, a low life expectancy, high rates of infant mortality, and an overall lack of safety and stability. In a world of plenitude, many people do not have enough to survive.

Wars are fought in the interest of the wealthy for the gain of the wealthy. War's primary victims are the poor of the countries that are invaded and the poor of the United States. Children are especially vulnerable. — The Poor People's Campaign.

How did we end up with such an unhealthy economic situation? Can an extremely unequal society also be a healthy society?

Capitalism is a term that refers to an economic system characterized by private ownership of the means of production. Capitalism represented a transformation from the previous system of feudalism (monarchs, lords, and nobility owned the land). Socialism is a newer term that advocates that the means of production, distribution, and exchange should be owned or regulated by the community (most often resulting in government control over the people's economic lives).

Feudalism, capitalism, and socialism are amoral market systems: they are not inherently immoral or moral. They differ about who owns what and how capital or goods are exchanged. However, capitalism and socialism have become ideologies imbued with robust belief systems. Since they have become ideologies, they serve as surrogate religions.

Today, capitalism has infected the world's largest religion, Christianity, forming a religious ideology distinct from the origins of Christianity and capitalism. One scholar coined the term "Evangelical-Capitalist Resonance Machine" (Connolly) to describe the unholy alliance between evangelicals and monopolistic capitalism. The followers of this movement do not follow the teachings of Jesus Christ, and they do not follow the fundamentals of capitalism. Jesus taught love, compassion, inclusion, and generosity. Capitalism dominated by global monopolies is not Adam Smith's capitalism. Unregulated monopolies have a detrimental impact on main street small businesses.

Freedom to initiate economic activity to compete with existing products and services is fundamental to true capitalism. Monopolies are anti-capitalism. Capitalism is not inherently driven by extreme greed but has developed into an economic and political belief system that suppresses competition and freedom. More than that, monopolistic capitalism does not believe in free markets; it believes in using power to make the market work for the benefit of monopolies.

The Evangelical-Capitalist Resonance Machine has morphed into the White Christian Nationalist (WCN) movement. The media has inadvertently aided the Un-Christian, greedy, judgmental, and violence-prone religious extremists by mislabeling them with the word "Christian." The Greek meaning of the word evangelical is "the good news" or "gospel." The problem is these religious extremists are not spreading good news, love, or compassion, so they are not following the teachings of the great Evangelist (Jesus). No wonder millions of loving, compassionate, and generous followers of the teachings of Jesus have left organized religion. The fastest-growing religious group is now the "nones" (no religious affiliation).

Once the multi-national capitalists gain complete domination over nations, those nations become plutocracies or autocracies. The citizens of nations are weak and powerless because the plutocrats unduly influence their elected leaders. The laws promoted by the WCN movement do not align with the teachings of Jesus, the Hebrew Prophets, or the values of the earliest Christians. The WCN movement does not welcome the stranger, and they do not love their enemies. The only term in the title "White Christian Nationalist" that fits is the term "White."

Every single one of the major world faiths, whether we're talking about Hinduism, Buddhism, Confucianism, Darwinism, Judaism,

Christianity, and Islam, have all come to the conclusion that what holds us back from our better self is ego, selfishness, greed, unkindness, hatred. And it all springs from a sense of thwarted ego.
— Karen Armstrong

The role of religion in a civil society is to maintain compassion and love for the neighbor. Religion should cultivate and encourage the goodness inherent in every human being, but it has far too often fueled the evil or shadow side of the human.

The earliest agrarian societies and most indigenous societies experienced cycles of abundance and scarcity because of nature's unpredictability. These were shared economic realities. However, as civilization developed, hierarchies of power soon followed. Economic inequality became entrenched in the culture as Kings and Priests instituted laws that demanded that people tithe or make sacrifices to them, whether there was enough left for the peasants or not.

The Middle Ages were a time when culture and knowledge regressed. Feudalism was the dominant economic and political system. Lords, kings, nobles, and clergy formed a hierarchy of power over the masses of people. Life was tough. People lived in small subsistence villages. Serfs and peasants stole food because food was often scarce. Feudal Lords demanded obedience from their serfs (the peasant class). Serfs were enslaved persons or tenant farmers. They did not own their land. They worked the land, and their Lord received part of the crops. Most of the wild game animals were owned by the Lords, and it was illegal for peasants to hunt without explicit permission. Drunken brawls, rapes, and mass killings were also commonplace. The honor and shame culture fueled extreme violence motivated by revenge. Homicide levels were at least ten times what they are today. Wars between neighboring lords were common. Serfs were obligated to serve in their lord's army. Sometimes, they could earn their freedom, become nobles, or even be "knighted" and allowed to wear heavy armor and lead the other peasants as a reward for bravery and exceptional fighting skills. Later in the Medieval period, the nature of warfare expanded and developed between emerging Nations. Although most of these wars were short (a few hours to a few days), the Hundred Years War (1337-1453) between England and France occurred toward the end of the Middle Ages. These wars were fought by the poor and powerless (often under duress) to protect the property rights of the Lords and Kings.

In the chapter on Religious Influences, we explored the intersections between the historical evolution of religion and ideologies. Market ideologies have developed in partnership with religious ideologies.

Monotheism and feudalism have the same roots. Feudalism is an economic system in which the means of production are owned and controlled by lords, kings, and priests (all of whom derive their power from God). It was the dominant economic system until the Protestant Reformation.

The Reformation was a time of massive transformation in all aspects of society. The population increased, villages grew, and more urban areas developed. Advancements in transportation and shipping created larger markets. Peasants moved to cities, learned new trades, and joined guilds. As the power of monarchs and the Church declined, mercantilism became the dominant economic system. Mercantilism was an economic ideology designed to generate greater wealth by increasing exports. Mercantilism motivated colonial expansion. An empire (with many locations) was more competitive in the trade wars than a single nation. The empires extracted raw materials from their subjects and sold them finished goods (at a profit to the empire). Indigenous people became another commodity to be exported, creating the slave trade.

As the economic inequality of a nation increases, the probability of violence and revolution increases. The Boston Tea Party protested mercantilism and economic inequality. Taxation without representation was not new, but the American colonists raised it as a primary political issue. For the English colonists, the tea tax violated their rights as Englishmen to "no taxation without representation."

Capitalism was already emerging in England among the landed aristocracy due to the early stage of the Industrial Revolution. New technologies led to the building of large factories and shifted the balance of power from the "Landed Aristocracy" to the new industrialists. Investing in factory buildings, machines, and equipment required substantial capital, not just for a growing season but for decades. The combination of the Industrial Age and the decline of the power of monarchs forced the transition from feudalism to mercantilism and eventually to corporate capitalism.

Colonization and mercantilism had devastating impacts on regions of the world where indigenous people practiced a gift economy. With a gift economy, you give, and you receive, and you receive, and you give. A gift economy can include bartering, reciprocal trade, or sharing. Plenitude is a characteristic of a gift economy. Gift economies emphasize interdependency, honor, loyalty, and intangible social rewards for generosity. European settlers did not understand that way of living. They arrogantly assumed their exploitive market ideologies were superior.

Once the colonizers had control of the new lands, they could own their land, tools, and machines and were free to produce goods and services. The economic system gradually shifted from mercantilism to capitalism as the power and influence of the monarchies decreased. Early capitalism offered the freedom to engage in productive work, the freedom to start and operate new enterprises, and the freedom to acquire and own land.

I believe that all lives have equal value. That all men and women are created equal. That everyone belongs. That everyone has rights and everyone has the right to flourish. I believe that when people who are bound by the rules have no role in shaping the rules, moral blind spots become law, and the powerless bear the burden. ... I believe that entrenched social norms that shift society's benefits to the powerful and its burdens to the powerless not only hurt the people pushed out but also always hurt the whole. — Melinda Gates

The extent of economic inequality goes through cycles. The years leading up to the 1929 Wall Street crash and the Great Depression are called the Gilded Age. During the Gilded Age, working conditions were unhealthy and dangerous. Monopolies developed and used their power to eliminate or eliminate competition. We experienced less inequality in the early post-World War II decades because wealth and income were taxed at high enough rates to redistribute the wealth more equitably. Money is power. Extreme economic inequality empowers the greedy and disempowers the poor. Between 1980 and 2020, economic inequality reverted to the extremes of the Gilded Age. Poverty has increased, and a large percentage of middle-class households are a few months away from falling into poverty or homelessness due to the loss of a job, a significant medical expense, or even the breakdown of their car.

During the COVID-19 pandemic, the mortality rates were five times higher for adults living in lower socioeconomic conditions. Because economic status and racial/ethnicity correlate, Hispanic, Black, Asian, and Indigenous populations experienced higher mortality rates. The COVID-19 mortality rate was lowest for wealthy white women. People who were privileged enough to either make ends meet for months without a job or to work from home could more easily ignore the public health warnings and even protest the restrictive policies, including mask requirements. Extreme differences in wealth and privilege conflicted with survival needs and fueled our divisions.

Capitalism is not inherently problematic. If politics support individual freedom and free enterprise, capitalism encourages entrepreneurship and small business. When the culture supports and promotes competition, capitalism offers the greatest freedom of the economic systems. In a free market, consumers choose among competing businesses. True capitalism requires a culture of political freedom and fairness in distributing wealth or profits. True capitalism allows workers to choose their employers and consumers to choose the products, services, and companies they do business with. The form of capitalism currently dominant in the United States is not free market capitalism. It has sometimes been called late capitalism. Others have pointed out the impact of the shift from capital, land, and labor to knowledge as the new basis of wealth.

In 1993, Peter Drucker predicted the shift to a post-capitalist economic system would be completed between 2010 and 2020. We could refer to the current economic system as "Terminal Capitalism." Terminal Capitalism is a market system that only values return on investment for CEOs (and the minority of shareholders with control of corporations) while placing no value on human beings (human resources), other animals, ecosystems, or the viability of life on earth.

The Supreme Court of the United States Citizens United decision fuels Terminal Capitalism by granting legal entities all the rights of living human beings without any of the responsibilities. Corporations have the right to control our political system, pollute, oppress workers, and cause harm to people and the environment. Corporations can buy control of our water. Corporations can purchase thousands of homes as investments, causing a massive housing crisis for workers and families.

When corporations market products that result in deaths, there are almost no consequences to the individuals making the decisions that cause the deaths. The corporations may suffer legal consequences, including damages, penalties, and fines. If people commit the same crimes as corporations, they can be incarcerated. Many states have death penalties for people who knowingly kill masses of people. Perhaps corporations should be dissolved/terminated if they cause multiple deaths, with the proceeds of the sale of the corporate assets funding a trust for the benefit of the victims of their corporate negligence.

In our research, we see a clear link between increased inequality and privileged groups support of societal hierarchies. This support is, in turn, linked to racism and increased willingness to take part in violent persecution of groups such as immigrants. The findings point to the possibly serious consequences of increased inequality because of the corresponding changes in the way people think and feel about social relations. — Lotte Thomsen

Capitalism, in its original form, contributed to a more equitable society. However, that is no longer the situation. We are extremely divided in terms of our access to the resources we need to sustain our lives. Yet, an extremely small number of humans have acquired wealth and power beyond that of any previous monarchs. The billionaire technology CEOs are the Masters of our Universe, not only because of their current estimated wealth but also because they collect private data and use it to manipulate and control us. If they have monopolistic power, most people are very vulnerable to their greed.

The Renaissance began during times of political and religious turmoil. A New Renaissance could transform the Evangelical-Capitalist Resonance Machine (White Christian Nationalism), one of our clear and present wicked challenges.

If we want to create a global economy that works for all living things, we must stop admiring the greediest CEOs at the top of our economic and political power pyramid. Instead, we need to boycott the monopolistic corporations and choose other options that support open-source technology. When we spend our time working for these harmful corporations, we are participating in the harm they do. When we spend our money with monopolistic corporations, we are participating in the harm they do. They could not exist without our time and money.

We still can boycott or choose not to participate in the schemes of our economic oppressors. We can choose different career paths. This could change because powerful corporate lobbyists are already asking for legislation and court rulings that will restrict our right to decide how we spend or invest our money and restrict our right to unionize and fight for better working conditions. Our future depends on defending and protecting these fundamental rights. Our future also depends on reclaiming our power and control over our personal data, the social media we use, and our DNA. When we choose open-source technology platforms, we have more power and control.

We can discern that a movement is totalitarian because a strong man will control it. He will openly exhibit grandiose narcissistic traits (an unmistakable sense of entitlement, an exaggerated belief in their superiority, and an obsession with themselves). His malignant narcissistic traits (manipulative, obsessive, aggressive, malicious, and cruel) may be less obvious, especially to his followers.

We cannot experience our collective power when we participate in any totalitarian movement. The United States' culture, social media, and economic system (Terminal

Capitalism) depend a great deal on nurturing our narcissistic tendencies. As the world's dominant superpower, the United States also has a powerful influence on global culture.

If we nurture our children and raise them to use their power in collaboration with others, we can create a future where the majority of people understand shared leadership. Children raised in a culture of sharing, caring, creating, and critical thinking can create a world that works for all living things.

Divide and Conquer

Are politics always divisive? Is democracy or majority rule an unrealistic notion? Can human effort coalesce without hierarchies of power? Why should we care?

Today, the United States of America is deeply divided along ideological lines. Many of us (nearly a majority) fear there will be political violence or even a civil war during the upcoming election cycle (2024). Three out of four believe that the United States democracy is under threat. Nearly one in four voters believe that political violence may be justified to "save" the country. That is because approximately half of voters expect that the losing side will not accept their losses peacefully, and half expect there will be violence over the election results. As divided and fearful as we are now, we were even more divided in the period leading up to the United States Civil War. The end of the Civil War did not end our political divisions.

History teaches us that hierarchical power generally involves intentionally divisive strategies. The ancient Babylonians were early pioneers of the divide-and-conquer approach. The strategy was used by the Greek and Roman Empires and every empire since then.

"Divide-and-conquer" was needed for colonization. The colonizers only needed to convince about twenty percent of their subjects to assume power over the rest of their people. By recruiting a class of loyal subjects to rule over other tribespeople, the colonizers could rule from a distance and extract resources and wealth to benefit the ruling class and the empires engaging in colonization. The twenty percent were given special privileges as a reward for oppressing the other eighty percent. This is also how the United States was colonized, forcing native people off the land, importing enslaved people from colonized areas in Africa, and granting a minority of white men title to land and the opportunity to gain wealth and power.

After the violent revolt that seized the United States Capitol on January 6, 2021, to block the peaceful transfer of Presidential power, the United States is now viewed by the rest of the world as the most politically divided nation. The United States, the country that participates in and even leads wars (that have never been declared or authorized by the US Congress) in other regions of the world in the name of promoting democracy, has not been able to maintain peaceful democratic order within its borders. We will never experience the true nature of our existence (that we are connected, not separate) while we are engaged in military conflict. We will not fully experience our connection until we learn how to live without the extremely polarized political divisions that create the conditions for war or violent revolutions.

The birth of the United States and many other nations involved violence (wars or revolutions), but there were also positive motivations at play.

We hold these truths to be self-evident, that all men are created equal, that they are endowed by their Creator with certain unalienable Rights, that among these are Life, Liberty, and the pursuit of Happiness. — That to secure these rights, Governments are instituted among Men, deriving their just powers from the consent of the governed. — Declaration of Independence

The Declaration of Independence proclaimed an ambitious and inspiring vision. However, the United States has never really been united, and all people are still not treated equally. We have always been divided. The United States has never lived up to the ideals of the Declaration of Independence. Yet, the Declaration of Independence is still one of the best examples of powerful political prose. Its purpose was to inspire the masses to take up arms and declare independence from the King of England (from the monarchy). The objective was twofold: to "declare" the causes or factors that justified the revolt and to inspire the people to break free from the British Empire.

Like many other nations, the United States was formed in the aftermath of a war. We started out colonizing land occupied by indigenous tribes. The United States was born through violence and division. Should we ever expect anything else?

The Preamble of the Declaration of Independence consists of a lengthy single sentence.

*When in the Course of human events, it becomes **necessary** for one people to dissolve the political bands which have connected them with another, and to assume among the powers of the earth, the separate and equal station to which the Laws of Nature and of Nature's God entitle them, a decent respect to the opinions of mankind requires that they should declare the causes which impel them to the separation.*

The word "necessary" implied that breaking ties to the British Empire was impelled by fate or determined by natural laws beyond the control of human agents. The notion of necessity was so crucial to the drafters' intentions that it was used two other times, and the word continued to be used in other official documents after July 4, 1776. If a violent conflict is necessary, we respond as though not only our form of government but also our very lives are at stake.

It also stated, in the form of a declaration, that the Americans were "one people" and the British an "other." A clear and powerful statement of "us" versus "them." It conveyed the idea that breaking the relationship with England was a necessary step in human progress. It also conveyed the idea that Americans and Englishmen were two distinct peoples attempting to hide the fact that this was a civil war. We were killing our neighbors. One out of three colonists remained loyal to England. Our enemy was the status quo. Our enemy was Monarchy as a political system. Our anger was towards Colonization, being one outpost in a vast British Empire.

Declaring the British people as the "other" was scapegoating. It dehumanized one-third of the colonists. The revolution leaders thought this scapegoating language was needed to persuade foreign nations to provide support. The foreign nations were unlikely to provide support for civil war or insurrection. The Declaration of Independence was successful in energizing George Washington's troops. Most units in the Continental Army and the state's militias were integrated, with white Europeans, African Americans, and Native Americans serving side by side. Many southern enslavers promised their slaves freedom if they would join the fight. After the war was won, when the founders were ready to form a government, the promises of equality and freedom for people of color were not honored.

The United States Constitution is dramatically different from the Declaration of Independence. The Declaration of Independence's declaration of equality and unalienable rights for all, combined with the radical notion that governments should derive their just powers from the consent of the governed, inspired a grand experiment in democracy. However, the United States Constitution (enacted in 1787, more than eleven years later) codified a constitutional federal republic, not sovereignty of the people or true democracy. The Constitution is the supreme law of the United States. Citizens in a democracy can either directly or indirectly influence the government, while citizens in a republic can only indirectly influence the government through elected officials.

The drafters of the Constitution were power-holders, and they did not honor the Declaration of Independence's promise to create a nation where the leaders only governed by the consent (majority vote) of the governed. The U.S. Constitution established checks and balances partly because the founders did not trust majority rule by the governed. The three branches of the government (Executive, Legislative, and Judicial) are co-equal. This is supposed to prevent any one branch from becoming too powerful. The power of the voters is also limited. The people only had power over the House of Representatives, one of the three branches. Before 1913, Senators were not elected by popular vote; state legislatures elected them. The people still do not directly elect the President. The 'electors' have that power (the Constitution refers to 'electors' not "electoral college'). The original selection process for President and Vice President was nonpartisan, with the candidate receiving the most votes becoming President and the second-ranking candidate becoming Vice President.

The United States became a two-party political system with the enactment of the 12th Amendment in 1804. It consolidated the ticket, and candidates for President ran with a Vice President. The Electoral College does not have to elect the candidate who wins the popular vote. Five presidents were selected by the Electoral College who did not win the popular vote. The Electoral College shaped our government into an entrenched political duopoly that ignores the popular vote for president.

Although there have been many shifts in the two parties, the Electoral College makes it nearly impossible for a third party or independent candidate to become president. It also distributes power unequally, giving states with smaller populations more power. It is also the force behind the swing state phenomenon, where most attention goes to the most deeply divided states. The Electoral College has institutionalized the domination of the two-party system and the disenfranchisement of independent voters. A two-party duopoly is inherently divisive.

The impetus for the two-party system arose from the first effort to create a central federal bank. Thomas Jefferson worried that a national bank would create a culture that favored financiers and merchants over plantation owners and family farmers (who tended to be debtors). A central bank symbolized how a privileged class of capitalists oppressed the will of the common people. This division foreshadowed the rise of plutocracy, or the rule by the wealthy in the United States.

Although divide-and-conquer strategies have profoundly shaped human history, today, most modern democracies are not dominated by the two-party system. The first one hundred years of the United States enjoyed a multi-party system. The founders were deeply concerned about the role of political parties.

The Nixon/Watergate scandal and resignation in the early 1970s destroyed a generation of Americans 'trust in the political process. It also redefined the government and media relationship, creating a permanent adversarial relationship. It sowed seeds of distrust and discontent.

The United States is the only large democracy with a deeply entrenched two-party system. Income and wealth inequality are substantially higher in the United States than in other developed nations. The higher the inequality, the more likely we are to move from democracy toward plutocracy. Economic inequality fuels political division. Both parties manage political campaigns that are highly negative toward the opposing party. We no longer trust our politicians, and our deep distrust of the candidate of the other party has become open hostility.

Since the Citizens United SCOTUS decision in 2010, the balance of power has tipped towards the wealthiest one percent. However, most partisan voters do not know that their adversary is not the Democrats or the Republicans. Our common adversary is the billionaires and the corruption of their money in our politics. There is no center in a plutocracy; instead, a small percentage is at the top of the economic pyramid calling the shots.

There are progressive billionaires, conservative billionaires, and libertarian billionaires. Recently, more billionaires have openly displayed and supported fascist ideologies. There is no consensus political view among the plutocrats. In smaller rural states like Montana, Wyoming, Idaho, and North and South Dakota, aspiring plutocrats can easily move into the state and use their money to gain powerful positions as senators or governors.

Dark money refers to spending to influence elections, public policy, and political discourse, where the source of money is not disclosed to the public. Although it is impossible to know the full extent of dark money, it is estimated that more than $1 billion was spent in 2020 at the federal level alone. The two parties point fingers at each other, claiming the other party receives more dark money. The reality is that the Republican Party and Democratic Party are both under the influence of plutocrats (through direct and open donations and dark money).

During extraordinary prosperity, we're also living through a crisis. Our communities are collapsing, and people are feeling more isolated, adrift, and purposeless than ever before. —Senator Ben Sasse

Loneliness and isolation are lingering effects of the COVID-19 pandemic. We also live with ever-present mortal threats (climate disasters and nuclear war). Americans sense that their elected representatives are out of touch. To make matters even worse, nearly sixty percent of Americans have no confidence that the two dominant parties can overcome their divisions and craft bipartisan solutions.

Trust in the Federal Government also hovers near a historical low. In October 2023, the approval rating of the United States Congress hit a historic low, dropping to thirteen percent (statista.com). Confidence and trust in the U.S. Supreme Court have declined to their lowest point since 1987. The Court's favorability rating has declined by 26 percentage points since 2020. These general statistics mask profound partisan differences. Democrats and Republicans don't agree about much of anything anymore. Both parties look at independents and third-party members as threats.

Many do not feel empowered under the two-party system. We may blame the other party or blame the two-party system itself (true for many independents), but we need to work together to take our power back from the plutocrats. We are divided by the corporations that hold monopolistic power over our daily lives. The threats to our well-being and security are not from the left or the right, from the Red States or the Blue States. Our most significant threats come from the top of the wealth and power hierarchy.

We experience anxiety, distrust, and fear as the signs of civil unrest increase. We wonder if our neighbor two doors down the street will someday come to steal the food and water we have stored in our basement in the event of a disaster that disrupts our economy. We may be afraid to go to the polls and vote when there are people with masks and guns guarding entry to the polling booth. We are scared we might die during a complication of pregnancy or we might have to bear our rapist's child. We may blame the refugees at the southern border, the liberals for funding our social safety net, or the conservatives for cutting government funding, but the real issue is the increasing concentration of wealth and power at the top of the pyramid.

Many are not proud of our country. We may not admit it to anyone but our closest family members and friends, but we struggle to find hope amid existential threats. Social media, television, and news sources feed our divided experiences. There is no consensus surrounding the daily news. A deeply entrenched two-party electoral system is inconsistent with the very notion of the word United. The billionaire-owned news sources easily divide us, so we cannot be united. The Citizens United SCOTUS ruling cleared the way for corporations to make unlimited and even undisclosed political contributions. A corporation may deduct political contributions equal to twenty-five percent of its taxable income. However, they primarily funnel their political contributions through super PACs and nonprofit organizations (Dark Money). Ironically, one of the biggest catalysts for our increasingly divisive politics came from a hypocritical source of dark money named Citizen's United. The organization's website still pretends its purpose is to give citizens control, but it consistently acts to divide the citizens of the United States.

We are told to blame the other - the person of color, the guy who carries his gun everywhere he goes, the immigrant or refugee, the LGBTQ community, the Democratic Party, or the Republican Party. We have cooperated with systems designed to disempower us.

The United States of America feels like it is coming apart. Extreme economic inequality creates a chasm between the rich and the poor, disintegrating our once-strong middle class. There are also deep cultural divides between urban and rural communities. Rather than merely disagreeing on the issues and policies, the two parties attempt to persuade us to view the opposition as evil. Candidates rarely emphasize their positions on issues, and most political spending focuses on demonizing the opposition candidate and inciting fear if an evil candidate is elected.

Although we feel the tension of division, we are not divided; we are united in a web of interdependency. We are stronger united than we are divided. It is time to close the divide, gather, and seek common values. Rather than base our votes on fear of the other party or candidate, we need to seek unbiased information about the candidate most likely to develop a unifying vision that can bring both parties together.

We voters need to know about candidates' positions on issues that impact our lives. Issues of concern for the majority of voters include:

- Our declining standard of living is not the same as what the news media covers as the "economy." The costs of the basics of life—housing, food, childcare, healthcare, and energy—have been increasing faster than wages and compensation. These are the components of working families' real economy.

- Affordable access to health care for everyone. Only three in ten adults have employer coverage. Three in ten adults are struggling to pay off debt from medical, eye, or dental care despite having insurance. The majority of insured adults have experienced problems in accessing medical treatments because their insurance controls access to care recommended by their medical provider. Most Americans think it is wrong that we pay more for medications than other developed nations.

- Equal rights. Patriarchy is the linchpin of all forms of oppression. If men are not superior to women, the entire power pyramid collapses. The pro-life movement should be called the anti-equality movement. The anti-abortion movement has never exhibited concern about protecting life. It is about controlling women's lives and bodies. Six out of ten voters say abortion should be legal in all or most cases. The vast majority of voters support access to birth control and first-trimester abortions. Most Americans disagree with the Supreme Court's Dobbs decision.
- Most voters support common sense gun control and view current US gun policy as dangerous.

These issues have support from a significant majority of U.S. voters, yet very little progress has been made to address them. Why? Mainly because the pharmaceutical industry, health insurance industry, billionaire CEOs, the NRA, and gun manufacturers unduly influence our elected leaders.

The lack of regulations to prevent corporations and billionaires from manipulating and controlling our elected representatives is at the root of our dissatisfaction with our leaders and our inability to progress on the issues that the majority cares the most about. The Citizens United Decision legalized political corruption. This is not democracy. This is plutocracy.

Everything is un-American that tends either to government by a plutocracy or government by a mob. To divide along the lines of section or caste or creed is un-American. All privileges based on wealth and all enmity to honest men merely because they are wealthy are un-American, both of them equally so. The things that will destroy America are prosperity-at-any-price, peace-at-any-price, safety-first instead of duty-first, the love of soft living, and the get-rich-quick theory of life. — Theodore Roosevelt

We need to hold our elected leaders accountable. Our votes should emphasize the character of the candidate. We should also demand they publish their official positions on the most critical issues before the election. After they are elected, we need grassroots advocacy to encourage them to honor their commitments and their responsibility to represent us. In short, we need a new experiment in democracy. We need a system of government that honors our right to vote and regulates campaign finance so that we know exactly where the money is coming from.

Our Wicked Challenges

Zeitgeist is originally a German word — Zeit means time, Geist means spirit, and the "spirit of the time" is what is going on culturally, religiously, or intellectually during a specific period. It represents the values, beliefs, and priorities shared by a group of people at a given time. Our dominant paradigms create our zeitgeist.

The zeitgeist of our current age is Paradox, a paradigm of contradiction, conflict, ambiguity, confusion, and division.

We have bigger houses but smaller families, more conveniences but less time.

We have more degrees but less sense; more knowledge but less judgment; more experts but more problems.

More medicines but less healthiness.

We've been all the way to the moon and back but have trouble crossing the street to meet our new neighbor.

We built more computers to hold more copies than ever but have less real communication;

We have become long on quantity but short on quality.

These are times of fast foods but slow digestion;

Tall men but short characters;

Steep profits but shallow relationships.

It's a time when there is much in the window but nothing in the room. — Rev. Dr. Bob Morehead

No wonder we feel divided. Our current zeitgeist is Paradox, and therefore, we struggle to resolve our wicked challenges. Wicked challenges are complex and ambiguous. Our intense conflicts and divisions make it difficult to agree on solutions. Our confusion makes it difficult to define the nature of the wicked challenges. Our tendency to think about right and wrong, good and evil, and true and false prevents us from discovering what is possible.

Wicked challenges are difficult to define because they are viewed differently by various stakeholders. In previous Chapters, we have presented a short list of potential wicked challenges to consider.

- Chaos caused by the climate crisis, extreme weather events, and human migration.
- Rising totalitarianism.
- Violence, mass shootings, and endless international military conflicts.
- Battles over control of public education and book-banning.
- Religious extremism and violence.
- Scapegoating.
- Extreme economic inequality, homelessness, hunger, and lack of access to health care.

Experimentation and "trial and error" approaches to address wicked challenges involve irreversible and possibly devastating effects. There is no end to the number of possible solutions to a wicked challenge. Just because wicked challenges are intimidating does not mean they cannot be resolved. We begin by avoiding the problem/solution paradox.

Much of what has been written about wicked challenges is ineffective because it starts by describing the wicked challenge as a problem. The problem-solution paradox states that we cannot think about solutions until we understand the problem, and we cannot understand a problem until we think about solutions. Wicked problems always involve paradox. To resolve the paradox, we need to think at a meta-level. When we avoid problems, our creativity is restricted. If we seek solutions, we are focused on problems, not possibilities. Problem-solution thinking is always cyclical.

How are we supposed to address wicked challenges? We begin by discovering the Wicked Questions underlying the challenge. The purpose of our Wicked Questions is not to find a single answer but to open a conversation about seemingly paradoxical realities that exist side-by-side.

We gather diverse minds and ask, how can we…? We gather diverse perspectives, knowledge, and experience and identify a paradoxical challenge for the group to confront. We identify a challenge, then list everything we know is true or believe to be true about the topic we have chosen. Then, we generate pairs of opposites or pairs with creative tension between two or more perspectives. Then, the group wrestles with the opposition or creative tension to develop powerful questions like:

- How can side one and side two both be true?
- How is it that we are side one and side two simultaneously?
- How can we (try this) … while also allowing (another idea…?

Conversation Cafés (conversationcafe.org) are powerful events for bringing larger groups together for small roundtable conversations. Sitting in circles with a simple set of conversation agreements and a talking object, small groups (between 5 and 7 people) engage in consecutive rounds of dialogue. These small group conversations invite people to listen to one another and reflect on a wicked challenge. This process can also be done virtually using facilitated breakout rooms instead of tables and virtual whiteboards instead of large poster-size paper.

After several rounds of these conversations (with people rotating to new small groups), the larger group debriefs the process with a series of questions:

- What have you seen, heard, and observed that stood out?
- Why is that important?
- What patterns or conclusions are emerging?
- Now what? What actions make sense?

The Conversation Cafe concludes with a process that defines "fifteen percent solutions," a structure that intends to trigger significant change by starting small. Frequently, a 15% solution involves changes that we (as individuals or small groups) can make to contribute to a more significant change. We can take these incremental steps without approval or resources from others. "Fifteen percent solutions" work best when groups work together to identify contributions to shared purposes or challenges.

Wicked challenges cannot be addressed within a hierarchical conversation. The more power a leader has over others, the weaker their decision-making ability. The wicked challenge of the Zeitgeist of Paradox is hierarchical power.

Centralized decision-making will never resolve our divisions and conflicts. We need an intersectional zeitgeist.

Instead, we are caught in a collection of "isms." Our toxic isms include racism, sexism, ageism, ableism, heterosexism, classism, antisemitism, cronyism, cynicism, imperialism, terrorism, and nationalism. We also deal with arguments about capitalism, socialism, and communism - three competing market ideologies. Our competing "isms" fuel our culture wars. The inherent paradox of the anti-woke movement is absurd; we cannot be intolerant of tolerance without being intolerant.

The word anti-racism suggests we are fighting racist people (us versus them). Dismantling racism suggests all of us, victims of racism and people who are complicit in racist systems, must work first to dismantle the aspects of our shadow that benefit from or support racism. Our "isms" often create and sustain our divisions and our "us versus them" perspectives.

What we need is consilience. Consilience is the jumping together of knowledge or the linking together of principles from different perspectives or disciplines. Conversation Cafes are consilience events. Consilience is not the same as consensus. Consilience is challenging because it is outside of traditional academic disciplines. It undermines deeply held biases or presumptions. Consilience moves us out of our neatly categorized and divided worldviews. Consilience requires a transformation of our educational paradigms. We no longer need educators to use didactic teaching methods to fill young minds with facts. Consilience is necessary to support a culture of We, not Us versus Them.

Envisioning Our Future

We sometimes think history is the story of gradual human evolution and progress. Human progress has not been a smooth, uphill climb. We make progress, and then we regress. We are simultaneously resistant to change and open to transformation. Change is incremental and based on the current situation. We change some aspects of the status quo to make it bigger, smaller, better, faster, and always some "other." We think change will create a future distinct from the past, but it doesn't.

In contrast to change, transformation represents a breakthrough from the constraints of the past. Transformation is a dramatic shift into a different form like the caterpillar becoming a butterfly or an egg becoming a bird. Transformation is a miraculous process, the result of which represents a departure or breakthrough from the past. History proves that human beings regress and progress. Evolution is not a nice linear uphill climb.

The culture of the Renaissance was dramatically different from that of the Middle Ages. The Renaissance was a transformational cultural movement that brought humanity from the Middle or Medieval Age to modernity. The Enlightenment was another era of cultural transformation that brought us the Industrial Revolution and the American, French, Haitian, Irishmen, Serbian, Latin American, and Greek Revolutions. During cycles of transformation, we imagine a future and invent ways to bring it about.

Change makes systems marginally better or worse. Transformation creates new systems and allows possibilities to emerge. We are in the middle of a transformative age. We are poised for another renaissance. Renaissance is a French word meaning rebirth. The future will be a dramatic departure from the recent past. Transformation often includes the destruction or death of the old ways of being and doing.

Zeitgeist refers to a generation's taste, outlook, spirit, and characteristics. Shifts in our zeitgeist (dominant paradigms) occur as individuals born within a generation reach maturity. The generation born after us (often our children) naturally has new, dramatically different worldviews that replace our ways of thinking and making sense of our world. We do not need to transform the zeitgeist of a specific generation; we only need to create the opportunity for the next generations to develop their zeitgeist. Our different generational zeitgeists explain why parents frequently have difficulty understanding our children's generation.

One of childhood's tasks is to imagine the future. Previous cultural transformations are correlated with children born during the decade before the transformation occurred. Children born with the gifts to transform their zeitgeist have shaped or influenced history. Generations are born with the traits needed to invent and create transformation from one age to the next. The births of generations of children transform zeitgeists.

Baby Boomers, the largest generation in history, created a highly narcissistic zeitgeist. Boomers were born into a generation with too many members, so they needed to compete for attention and resources. The Baby Boom generation has rightfully been labeled the "Me Generation." As Boomers retire and quit working, they will require more resources than any previous generation. There are wicked challenges to face as Boomers age.

When our children mature, they naturally create the zeitgeist of their time. We need to trust our younger generations and nurture them so that they manifest more of their positive aspects and avoid projecting their collective shadow in violent and destructive ways. Will we raise our children to create a world that works for all living things, or will we raise a generation of narcissists?

Whether you believe climate change is an existential threat or align yourself with climate change deniers, there is no denying the impacts of more frequent extreme weather events and natural disasters on our lives. These traumatic disasters negatively impact our mental health and increase the frequency of anxiety, depression, and suicide. Over the ten years leading up to the COVID-19 pandemic, reports of depression/sadness and suicidal thoughts and behaviors among youth increased by 40%. Our children are justifiably concerned about violence (especially school shootings), climate change, nuclear weapons, global violence, and political polarization. No wonder so many of our children and young adults suffer from depression and anxiety.

Humans survived other times of dramatic climate change that caused famine and contributed to plagues. We are surviving now, even though the cost of food increased dramatically between 2000 and 2023 (over 23% since the

COVID-19 pandemic). We will face more epidemics and even pandemics in the future.

Artificial intelligence and biotechnology advances will transform what it means to be human. Although it is too soon to know, Generation Z (1997-2012) is showing early indicators that their zeitgeist will include a strong sense of social justice (equality) and promoting diversity in all areas of society. We can be hopeful if we learn to trust human progress and evolution.

The Revolutionary War ultimately birthed the United States of America. The Age of Revolution (late 18th to mid-19th centuries) was not a time of change but a time of transformation. The Declaration of Independence inspired the paradigm shift needed to move the colonies from being subjects of the British Empire to a paradigm without lords or monarchs. Although the individuals involved are often called the "Founding Fathers," they were not old men. More than a dozen signers of the Declaration of Independence were 35 or younger. Thomas Jefferson was thirty-three. The average age was forty-four. In 2024, the average age of United States Senators is 65.3 years. It is not the older generations who will lead us to a viable future but the youngest leaders.

After the Industrial Age came the Information Age. The transformation, or the end of an Age, often begins when power becomes extremely concentrated. As the Information Age matured, power became more concentrated in technology monopolies. Like the dawn of the other two eras of dramatic social transformation (the Renaissance and Revolution), we are currently experiencing the dawning of a new age. Yet, most of us don't feel hopeful. Because transformation is less predictable than change, we feel anxious. The fossil fuel industry is fighting to stay alive and keep its power. Huge factories and fossil fuels are not our future.

2020 marks the end of the Information Age and the beginning of a new Era. Perhaps power self-corrects when the balance tips too far toward totalitarianism or fascism. When the strong man at the top of the power pyramid starts killing members of his inner circle because he feels they are a personal threat, the pyramid usually falls apart. 2020 - 2026 will be remembered as a dramatic, brief regression – a dark chapter in human history. Once again, power and wealth are extremely concentrated, and oppression and violence are out of control. The period of regression can be short, but only if we collaborate to envision and create another renaissance.

A renaissance for our times will not look like our past. Seeds, or imaginal cells, are present even in this dark moment of history. Younger generations are already showing up with fresh ideas. Older polymaths and creative thinkers are also currently nurturing seeds capable of resolving wicked challenges. We are in a chrysalis moment, which is dark, messy, and very uncomfortable. We can study human history to see other cycles, but history will not reveal the nature of our future breakthroughs and transformations. History reminds us that other Chrysalis times were followed by dramatic transformative progress.

We must imagine our shared future. Although civil society institutions are failing or disintegrating, the universe cycles, and human history cycles. We see evidence of birth, death, and rebirth everywhere in the natural world.

Impermanence and selflessness are not negative aspects of life but the very foundation on which life is built. Impermanence is the constant transformation of things. Without impermanence, there can be no life. Selflessness is the interdependent nature of all things. Without interdependence, nothing could exist. — Thich Nhat Hanh

As we live through the end of the Information Age, we now understand that having unlimited access to information has not resolved our wicked challenges. There is too much information available. When we need information, we Google it. However, we no longer know what is true and what is false. We have experienced the internet's benefits in connecting us and its harm and ability to increase divisions and violence. The internet depends on binaries or dualities (0s and 1s). We have become dependent on computers, smartphones, devices, and the internet, and they are all fundamentally built upon this binary logic. Information is now converted to bits and bytes of data.

The good news is that the information-rich world of the internet is fertile ground for the development of polymaths. The printing press contributed to the emergence of polymaths, resulting in the Renaissance. The printing press accelerated the spread of ideas and knowledge, increased literacy rates, and significantly impacted the arts. The printing press offered all sorts of new and exciting possibilities. Before the printing press, only the clergy were regular readers. The internet has a similar impact today. We are experiencing a new polymath renaissance. A polymath is an individual whose knowledge spans many varied and often unrelated subjects. Because of the breadth of their knowledge, polymaths are known to draw on complex bodies of knowledge to solve complex problems.

We are met with choices every day. Within each, we can choose the deep and narrow route; or we can choose the wide and shallow one. We can choose to know, or we can choose to see. We can drive to answers, or we can learn to question our questions to expand them. We can surround ourselves with people who make us feel better about ourselves, or who share our views about everything, or we can find those who challenge us to grow, or whose own thoughtfulness makes us wonder more, not less.

These things are all well within reach of every person on Earth. And while they might mostly be gone, we have polymaths to thank for all of it. —Anthony Fieldman

Polymaths see the world, process information, and experience life differently. They may or may not possess a depth of expertise in a single subject. Although the Industrial Age and Information rewarded specialization in knowledge and skills, cultural transformation requires creativity, imagination, and curiosity. Subject matter experts often cannot see the forest for the trees; polymaths can. Polymaths recognize patterns and interrelationships between ideas and understand complex systems.

As we explored in **Our Education**, we need to transform the nature of education from kindergarten to our Ph.D. programs so that we support polymathy. For example, a Ph.D. is typically a highly specialized degree requiring in-depth research and expertise in a specific area, usually with a narrow focus. We need to encourage more interdisciplinary Ph.D. programs capable of producing polymaths.

Consilience is defined as the jumping together of knowledge or linking principles from different disciplines to form more comprehensive theories. The origin of the word consilience (come + jump) is like resilience (jump + back).

Consilience supports resilience in our culture. We need consilience to create a culture of collaborative leadership. Multiple polymaths working with other people with in-depth specialized subject matter expertise creates a both/and approach capable of producing the consilience we need to address our collective wicked challenges. We need polymaths and specialists working collaboratively.

A 21st-century renaissance educational system needs a pedagogy of consilience, a societal emphasis on knowledge (depth and breadth), critical thinking, civic engagement, and empathy. The curriculum is the content used to teach in traditional education. Pedagogy is how you teach. A pedagogy of consilience would intentionally produce a society with the wisdom of polymaths and the subject matter depth of S.T.E.M., S.H.A.P.E., or Ph.D. programs.

The Anti-Woke and White Christian Nationalism movements would like to silence or destroy polymaths. These ideologies are a backlash against diversity and polymathy. The desire driving the paradigm (mindset) of White Christian Nationalism is the desire to separate and conquer. It is also a desire to concentrate and accumulate wealth and power. These movements use fear (they appeal to our shadows) and ask us to blame others (to project our shadow). Most adherents to this dangerous ideology are highly resistant to progress and terrified of transformation. It is a regressive ideology.

The White Christian Nationalist paradigm supports scapegoating and authoritarian leadership. Adherents mistakenly believe they are superior to others. They also believe their salvation depends on believing what their leaders tell them and obeying those leaders. They believe when their leader tells them their neighbor is vermin (not human). They cannot comprehend that their ideology is evil.

They don't know the truth. The truth is this: the line between good and evil strikes through the heart of every human being, even theirs.

Our Declaration of Interdependence

Our collective work is to cultivate our goodness. Together, we can create a culture of active hope. We are the leaders we have been waiting for. We can give birth to new paradigms. We are the New Renaissance People.

We need a Declaration of "We."

All human beings are born free and equal in dignity and rights. Our human rights are indivisible and inalienable. We are endowed with reason and conscience and should act toward one another in a spirit of interdependence. Therefore, we resolve and invite everyone to uphold and promote mutual consideration, respect, and dignity.

Together, we can give birth to a new renaissance capable of overcoming the existential threats we face. We face a daunting task. The future is ours to create. The time is now.

We are in this together. We are woven into the tapestry of the universe. Love is the most powerful force in the universe. Let this be true.

Please feel free to share this book widely.
It is published under a Creative Commons license.

Made in the USA
Columbia, SC
20 November 2024